✷ *A Joyful Noise* ✷

A Joyful Noise

Four Psalms

Henry Holt and Company
New York

❁ *Contents* ❁

Psalm 46

od is our refuge and strength,
a very present help in trouble.

Therefore will not we fear,
though the earth be removed,
and though the mountains be carried
into the midst of the sea;

Though the waters thereof roar
and be troubled, though the mountains
shake with the swelling thereof.
Selah.

here is a river,
the streams whereof
shall make glad
the city of God, the holy place of
the tabernacles of the most High.

God is in the midst of her;
she shall not be moved:
God shall help her,
and that right early.

11

he heathen raged,

the kingdoms were moved:

he uttered his voice,

the earth melted.

The Lord of hosts is with us;

the God of Jacob is our refuge.

Selah.

ome, behold
the works of the Lord,
what desolations he hath
made in the earth.

He maketh wars to cease
unto the end of the earth;
he breaketh the bow,
and cutteth the spear in sunder;
he burneth the chariot in the fire.

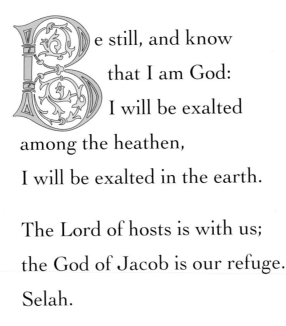

Be still, and know
that I am God:
I will be exalted
among the heathen,
I will be exalted in the earth.

The Lord of hosts is with us;
the God of Jacob is our refuge.
Selah.

he Lord is my Shepherd;
I shall not want.

He maketh me to lie down
in green pastures: he leadeth me beside
the still waters.

e restoreth my soul:

he leadeth me in the paths of

righteousness for his name's sake.

Yea, though I walk through the

valley of the shadow of death,

I will fear no evil:

for thou art with me;

thy rod and thy staff they comfort me.

hou preparest a table
before me in the presence
of mine enemies:
thou anointest my head with oil;
my cup runneth over.

Surely goodness and mercy
shall follow me all the days of my life:
and I will dwell in the house of the Lord
for ever.

Lord our Lord, how excellent
is thy name in all the earth!
who hast set thy glory above the heavens.

Out of the mouth of babes and
sucklings hast thou ordained strength
because of thine enemies, that thou
mightest still the enemy and the avenger.

hen I consider thy heavens,

the work of thy fingers,

the moon and the stars,

which thou hast ordained;

What is man,

that thou art mindful of him?

and the son of man,

that thou visitest him?

For thou hast made him
a little lower than the angels,
and hast crowned him
with glory and honour.

hou madest him to have dominion over the works of thy hands; thou hast put all things under his feet:

All sheep and oxen, yea, and the beasts of the field;

The fowl of the air, and the fish
of the sea, and whatsoever passeth
through the paths of the seas.

O Lord our Lord, how excellent
is thy name in all the earth!

ake a joyful noise
unto the Lord,
all ye lands.

Serve the Lord with gladness:
come before his presence
with singing.

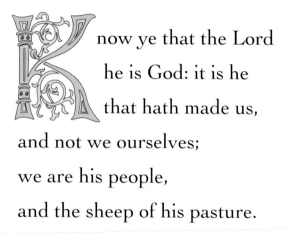

now ye that the Lord
he is God: it is he
that hath made us,
and not we ourselves;
we are his people,
and the sheep of his pasture.

Enter into his gates
with thanksgiving,
and into his courts with praise:
be thankful unto him,
and bless his name.

For the Lord is good;
his mercy is everlasting;
and his truth endureth
to all generations.

The Paintings

❀ Johan Christian Clausen Dahl ❀
Morning after a Stormy Night

Dahl was born in Norway, the son of a fisherman. People from his hometown recognized his artistic talent early on, and raised the funds to send him to the Copenhagen Academy. His painting quickly earned acclaim and, at the age of thirty, he moved to Dresden, where he lived the rest of his life. He was a close friend of Caspar David Friedrich and other German Romantic painters in Dresden. Despite his personal affinity for the members of this group, his exquisitely rendered landscapes have a much stronger connection to such Realist painters as Constable (see page 65).

Dahl considered *Morning after a Stormy Night* to be his best work. It clearly shows his stunning ability to paint in a naturalistic manner and it demonstrates his long-held fascination with portraying the effects of light and weather. While on the surface this is a shipwreck scene — a very popular genre at the time — Dahl was more interested in depicting the anguish attendant upon human tragedy.

Johan Christian Clausen Dahl, Norwegian, 1788–1857
Morning after a Stormy Night, 1819
Oil on canvas, 29 1/16 × 41 3/16 in. (74.5 × 105.6 cm)
Neue Pinakothek, Munich (inv. no. 14631)
(Details on pages 7 and 8)
Photograph: Joachim Blauel/ARTOTHEK

Anonymous Netherlandish Painter, 16th century
Landscape: A River among Mountains, ca. 1525–50
Oil on panel, 19 13/16 × 26 3/4 in. (50.8 × 68.6 cm)
National Gallery, London (NG 1298)
(Details on pages 11 and 17)

Anonymous Netherlandish Painter
Landscape: A River among Mountains

With centuries of landscape painting behind us, it is fascinating to recall that prior to the sixteenth century, landscape was not a usual subject for painters. While some of the most magnificent landscapes ever painted predate this work, they were backgrounds for religious, historical, or mythological subjects. This is one of the first works to make the depiction of landscape its primary purpose.

The poplar wood medium was a favorite of contemporary Italian artists; it has even been suggested that its author was an Italian enamored of Northern art. But this panel is indebted primarily to Pieter Bruegel: it is based on an engraving after a work by that great Netherlandish master.

The small figure under the tree paints the scene before him. Standing in for the viewer, he provides a point of view from which to take in this magical vista comprised of elements of the everyday, all swirled together in a delicate tribute to the marvels of nature.

❀ Philips Wouwerman ❀
Cavalry Making a Sortie from a Fort on a Hill

Of the three painter-brothers from Haarlem named
Wouwerman, only Philips went on to be counted among
the most popular painters in Holland, and avid interest in
his work lasted into the twentieth century. Seventeenth-
century Dutch painters tended to concentrate on specific
types or subjects of painting, and Philips Wouwerman's
fortes were landscapes populated by numerous small,
meticulously rendered figures and carefully observed,
exquisitely painted pictures of horses. Both of these
talents are apparent in this battle scene.

    At the time of this work's creation, artists were
usually required by their patrons to represent battles as
exemplary of heroism, courage, or brilliant strategy. But
since *Cavalry Making a Sortie* probably does not represent
a specific historic event, Wouwerman was free to depict
the destructive power and terrifying results of battle.

Philips Wouwerman, Dutch, 1619–68
Cavalry Making a Sortie from a Fort on a Hill, 1646
Oil on canvas, 54 3/16 × 74 5/16 in. (139 × 190.5 cm)
National Gallery, London (NG 6263)
(Details on pages 13 and 14)

❀ Jean-François Millet ❀
Shepherdess and Her Flock

Millet came from Normandy, but moved to Paris when he was twenty-three. There he became a follower of the then-traditional academic style. It wasn't long, however, before he turned his attention to subjects from country life. Rather than sentimentalizing these scenes, as many of his contemporaries did, Millet strove to depict them as aspects of human experience worthy of our notice. He is among the best-known and most widely admired French painters from the mid-nineteenth century; works like *The Gleaners* and *The Angelus* have been sources for popular prints ever since.

Millet's interest in portraying the sadness and poverty, as well as the dignity, inherent to contemporary rustic life is evident in this painting of a shepherdess, who pauses to reflect during one of many exhausting days of watching over her flock of sheep. At once melancholy and uplifting, it is not difficult to understand why this became Millet's first overwhelming success in exhibition.

Jean-François Millet, French, 1814–1875
Shepherdess and Her Flock, 1862–64
Oil on canvas, 31 9/16 × 39 3/8 in. (81 × 101 cm)
Musée d'Orsay, Paris (RF 1879)
(Detail on page 19)
Photograph: © PHOTO R.M.N.

❈ Hans Thoma ❈
The Rhine near Säckingen

Hans Thoma was born into a family of German laborers who lived in the Black Forest. He studied lithography and began his career as a painter by decorating watches and jewelry cases with miniatures. Trips to Italy and France had a tremendous impact on his art and he took great inspiration from the works of Gustave Courbet and Arnold Böcklin, among other nineteenth-century painters. His work enjoyed enormous popularity during his lifetime.

The Rhine near Säckingen demonstrates the influence Thoma derived from the works of French Impressionist painters, most notably Claude Monet and Charles-François Daubigny. Although here four figures comprise the peasant family shown in the foreground, this scene readily brings to mind traditional depictions of the Flight into Egypt. The mother protectively balances her baby on a donkey; her white headscarf and the infant's blond hair may even be read as hints of traditional halos.

Hans Thoma, German, 1839–1924
The Rhine near Säckingen, 1873
Oil on canvas, 24 3/4 × 43 7/8 in. (63.5 × 112.5 cm)
Staatliche Museen zu Berlin Preußischer Kulturbesitz,
Nationalgalerie
(Detail on page 20)

Jozef Israels, Dutch, 1824–1911
The Shepherd's Prayer, 1864
Oil on canvas, 35 3/16 × 48 15/16 in. (90.3 × 125.5 cm)
The Toledo Museum of Art, Toledo, Ohio;
Gift of Edward Drummond Libbey (14.116)
(Details on pages 22 and 25)

◉ Jozef Israels ◉
The Shepherd's Prayer

Although Jozef Israels began his career as an artist in Amsterdam and Paris painting portraits and historical subjects, he is best known for his images of peasants and fisherpeople. He was just ten years younger than Millet, and when one sees a painting like this, there is little wonder that Israels was dubbed "the Dutch Millet" (see page 54). After returning to the Netherlands, he settled in The Hague, where he became one of the leading members of the Hague School, which in many ways set about revitalizing the great Dutch tradition of the Golden Age.

The Shepherd's Prayer is quite typical of the paintings for which Israels is best known. Its sweetly sentimental depiction of the life of the peasantry sets it apart from the more monumental and stern images of Millet. But it also aptly conveys the concept that a firm belief in God and an understanding of nature make it possible to contend with the difficulties of country life.

⊛ John Linnell ⊛
The Storm (The Refuge)

John Linnell was a highly successful painter of portraits and miniatures, but his greatest affection was for landscape painting. From childhood, his affinity for the countryside spurred him to develop his talent at rendering its beauty, peace, and savagery. At the age of twenty-six he began his lasting friendship with William Blake, whose influence may be detected in Linnell's early landscapes. By the late 1840s, he was accorded the acclaim he sought as a landscapist, but his fellow English painters repeatedly rebuffed him in his quest for membership in the Royal Academy.

The stirring depiction of nature's raw power is found in many of Linnell's best landscapes, a quality that may stem from his deeply held religious beliefs. *The Storm* — other versions of which are entitled *The Refuge* — shows terrain near the home of the artist. His deft use of almost hallucinatory colors in the earth and the sky enables us to sense the moment of calm before a storm.

John Linnell, English, 1792–1882
The Storm (The Refuge), 1853
Oil on canvas, 35 5/8 × 57 5/8 in. (90.5 × 146.4 cm)
Philadelphia Museum of Art: The John H. McFadden Collection
(Details on pages 27 and 28)

❊ Caspar David Friedrich ❊
Woman at Sunrise

Friedrich is among the greatest of the Romantic painters. He was a close friend of Goethe, with whom he shared many ideas about spirituality and nature. Even the simplest sketch from this Dresden artist's hand is rife with his respect for God and nature, which he considered to be as one. Friedrich's paintings are imbued with paradox and symbolism and an overwhelming sense of reverence.

This is readily apparent in *Woman at Sunrise*. The woman, seen from the back, gives no clue as to her purpose as she stands before the rising sun symbolic of resurrection. Is she exulting in its beauty or stunned by its power? While the trees and mountain connect earth and heaven, they also emphasize the human experience of separation from heaven. The colors suggest that this is a deeply spiritual expression of the joy and the awe that transcendent moments of natural wonder can inspire. One of Friedrich's greatest works, it is also one of his most enigmatic.

Caspar David Friedrich, German, 1774–1840
Woman at Sunrise, ca. 1818
Oil on canvas, 8 3/4 × 11 3/4 in. (22 × 30 cm)
Museum Folkwang, Essen
(Detail on pages 30–31)

John Constable, English, 1776–1837
Wivenhoe Park, Essex, 1816
Oil on canvas, 22 1/8 × 39 7/8 in. (56.1 × 101.2 cm)
Widener Collection, National Gallery of Art,
Washington, D.C. (1942.9.10.(606)/PA)
(Detail on pages 36–37)
© 1995 Board of Trustees, National Gallery of Art

John Constable
Wivenhoe Park, Essex

Along with J.M.W. Turner, John Constable is generally credited with being the greatest of English landscape painters. The son of a wealthy mill and property owner, an economic position that allowed him to devote himself to art, he did not decide to become a painter until he was twenty-three. Unlike many artists, Constable never left England; his landscapes are of the scenes he knew well and loved intensely. He broke with tradition in many ways, such as his handling of light effects. This, and his inclination to work outdoors, would later influence the Impressionists at the end of the nineteenth century.

Constable wrote "[never] were there…two leaves of a tree alike since the creation of the world." *Wivenhoe Park, Essex,* is a testament to his interest in, and talent for, capturing the specific details of the landscape, not only in a documentary way, but also as an homage to the beauty and grandeur of nature and to the homeland he loved so well.

❀ Judith Leyster ❀
Boy Playing a Flute

The artist's life has seldom been an easy one, but it has
been infinitely more difficult for women until recently.
This is due in part to the fact that so little is known about
female artists from earlier times—what remain of their
works are often discounted as inferior or mistakenly
attributed to male artists. Thus, we are doubly fortunate
to find works of such high quality by Judith Leyster.

Leyster's talent was recognized and nurtured by her
family. She studied with Frans Hals and other masters, later
marrying Jan Miense Molenaer, a Dutch painter of genre
subjects, with whom she worked closely until her death.

Boy with a Flute is one of her most successful paintings.
Though the identity of the sitter is unknown, the percep-
tive manner in which Leyster rendered his facial features
and the sensitive handling of his posture as he performs
suggest that this work may be a portrait of a particular per-
son rather than a generic image of a music-making youth.

Judith Leyster, Dutch, 1609–60
Boy Playing a Flute, ca. 1630–35
Oil on canvas, 28 1/2 × 24 3/16 in. (73 × 62 cm)
Nationalmuseum, Stockholm
(Detail on page 39)

David Teniers the Younger, Flemish, 1610–90
The Artist with His Family, ca. 1645–46
Oil on panel, 15 3/16 × 22 5/8 in. (38 × 58 cm)
Staatliche Museen zu Berlin Preußischer Kulturbesitz,
Gemäldegalerie (cat no. 857)
(Details on pages 2 and 41)

❂ David Teniers the Younger ❂
The Artist with His Family

Although many members of the Teniers family of Antwerp
were painters, David the Younger was by far the best
known and most prolific. His specialty was genre scenes
centered on peasant life, but in his capacity as court painter
to—and curator of the collections of—Archduke Leopold
Wilhelm of Austria, he made a number of remarkable
canvases that record whole galleries hung with paintings.

Music-making was a favorite subject for seventeenth-
century Flemish and Dutch painters, but their images
often came freighted with an underlying tinge of raucous
revelry or of music as "the food of love." Thus Teniers's
choice of portraying his family making music is all the
more touching. In his hands, this becomes a tribute to
familial harmony and concord. The painter certainly knew
whereof he painted, for he was also a virtuoso at the viola
da gamba, the forerunner of the cello, which he is shown
playing in this self-portrait.

❀ Pieter Jansz. Saenredam ❀
St. Bavo in Haarlem

Architecture was a favorite subject for Dutch painting
and Saenredam was a master who painted little else. He
lived principally in Haarlem, home of the cathedral seen
here, and he frequently traveled to other cities in the Low
Countries to fulfill commissions for his exacting, elegant
pictures of buildings. While earlier Dutch painters primarily
showed a fanciful sort of architecture—a kind of "stage set"
in or around which their scenes took place—the compelling
interest for Saenredam was the structure itself, earning him
the moniker "the first portraitist of architecture." The clarity
of detail and documentary depiction in his paintings relies
heavily on his great talent for rendering perspective.

Saenredam painted several great pictures of St. Bavo,
the church in which he was later buried. Like many
Roman Catholic churches in Holland, it was purged of all
decorative detail when Calvinism took root. As a result,
their interiors are pristine, unadorned spaces, even today.

Pieter Jansz. Saenredam, Dutch, 1597–1665
St. Bavo in Haarlem, 1631
Oil on panel, 32 × 42 7/8 in. (82 × 110 cm)
Philadelphia Museum of Art: The John G. Johnson Collection
(Detail on pages 44–45)

Henry Holt and Company, Inc.
Publishers since 1866
115 West 18th Street
New York, New York 10011

Henry Holt® is a registered trademark of
Henry Holt and Company, Inc.

Published in Canada by Fitzhenry & Whiteside Ltd.,
195 Allstate Parkway, Markham, Ontario L3R 4T8.

Library of Congress Catalog Card Number: 95-80844

ISBN 0-8050-4648-8

Henry Holt books are available for special promotions and
premiums. For details contact: Director, Special Markets.

First Henry Holt Edition—1996

Designed by Peter M. Blaiwas

Printed in Singapore
All first editions are printed on acid-free paper. ∞

10 9 8 7 6 5 4 3 2 1